1 & 2 THESSALONIANS

1 & 2 THESSALONIANS

VERSE-BY-VERSE GRAPHIC NOVEL WEB TRANSLATION

ILLUSTRATIONS BY THOMAS FASANO

1 & 2 THESSALONIANS: VERSE-BY-VERSE GRAPHIC NOVEL WEB TRANSLATION

Illustrations Copyright © 2025 by Thomas Fasano

The World English Bible is in the public domain.

Published by Coyote Canyon Press
Claremont, California

ISBN: 979-8-9937072-1-1

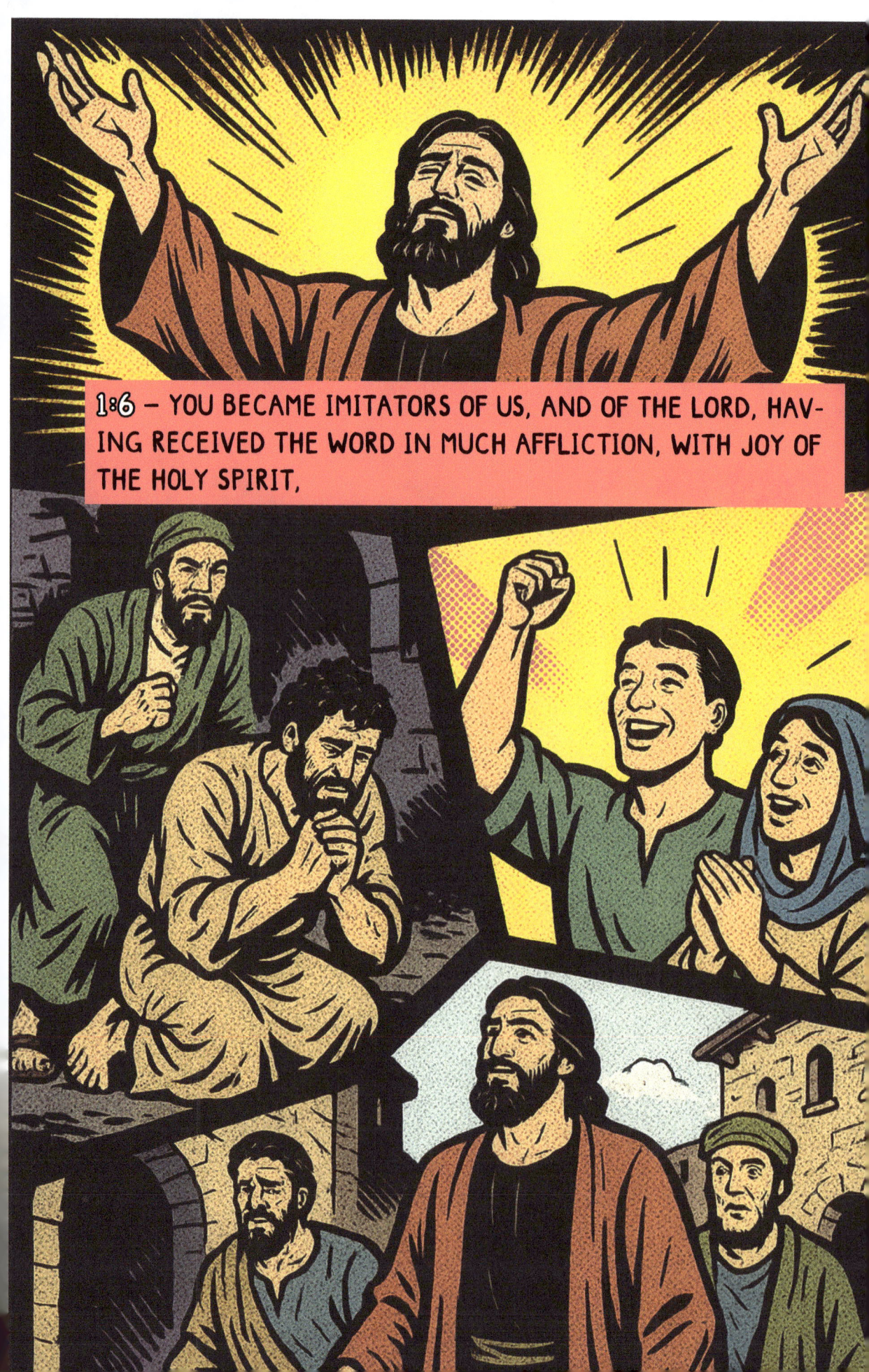

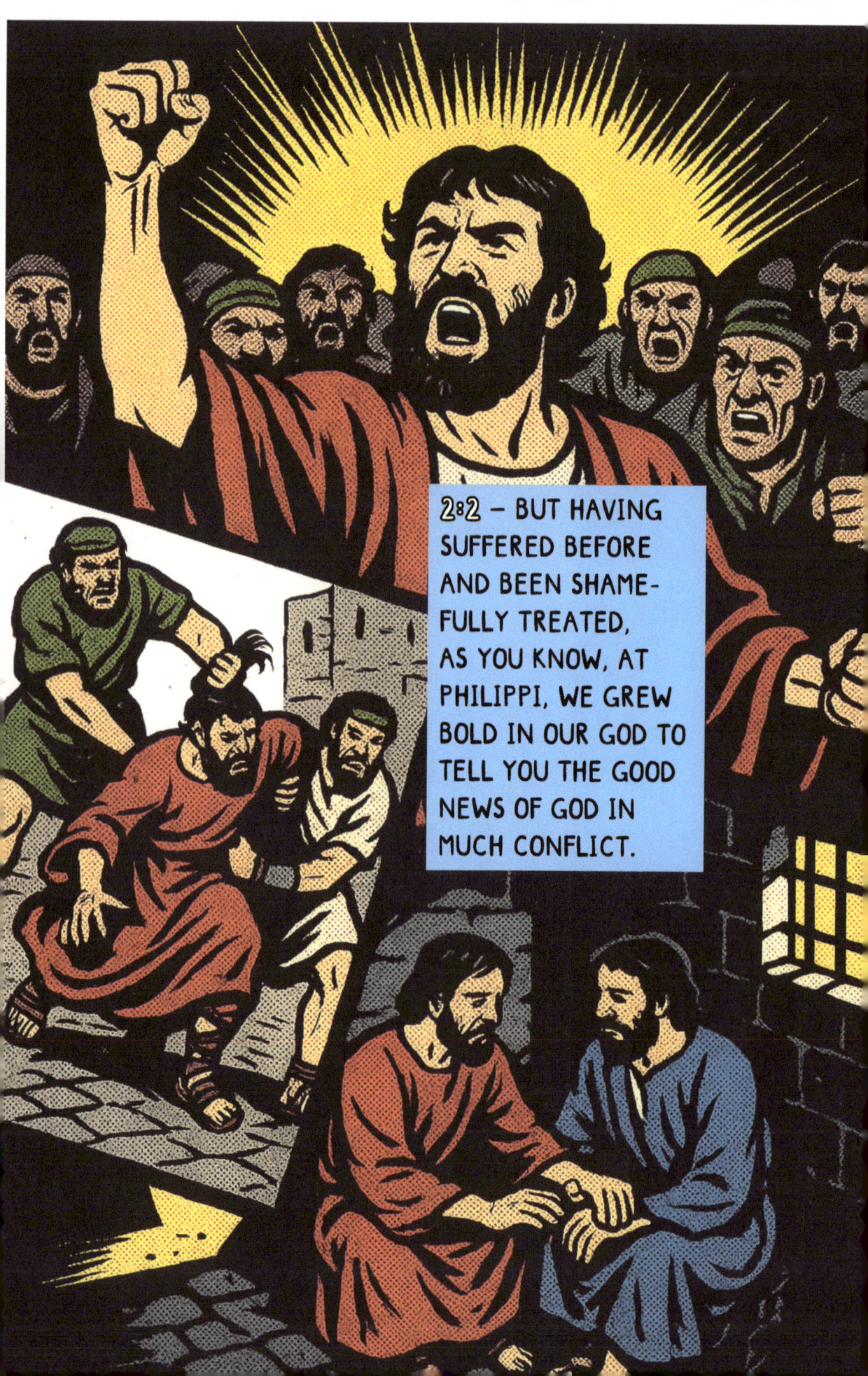

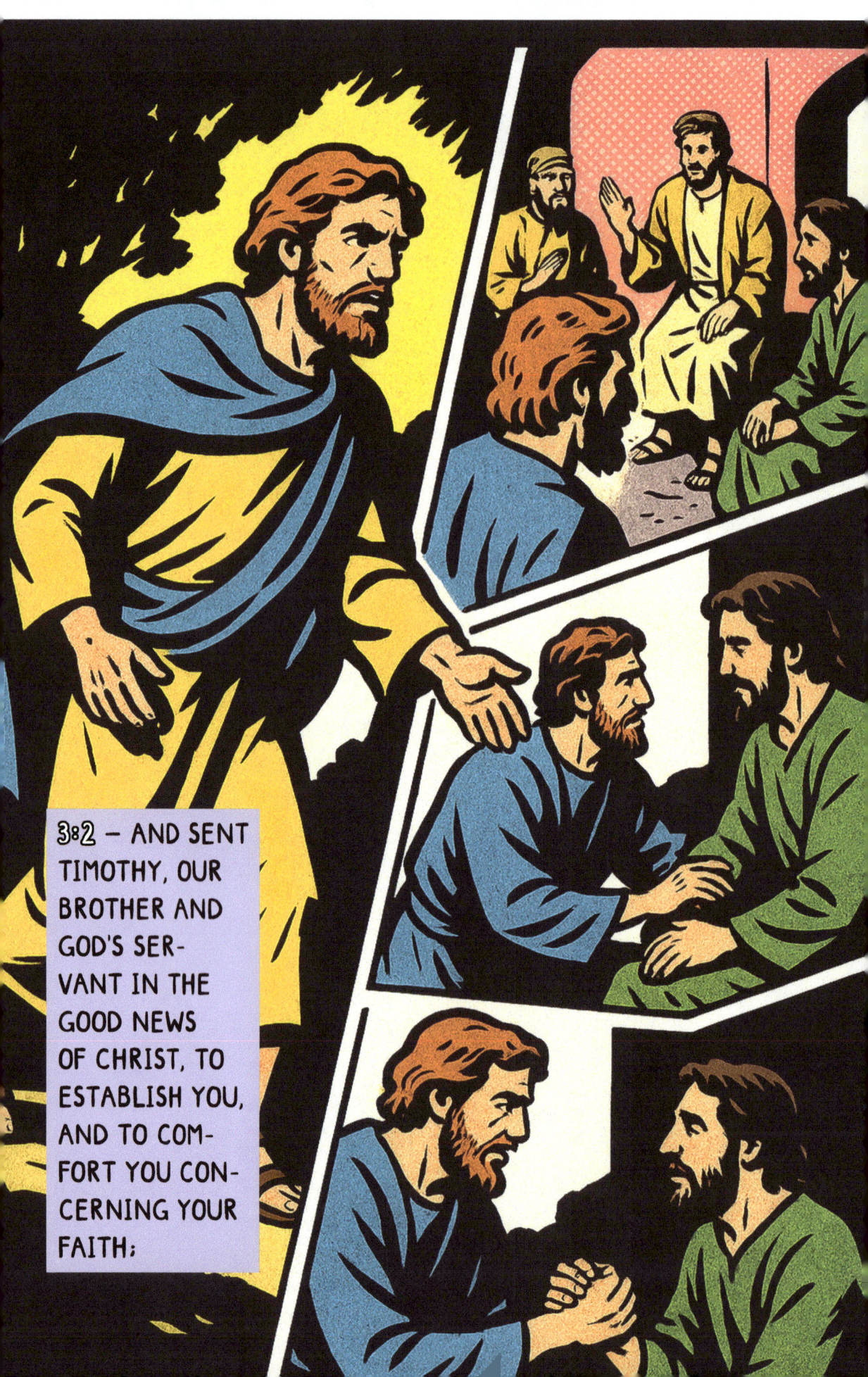

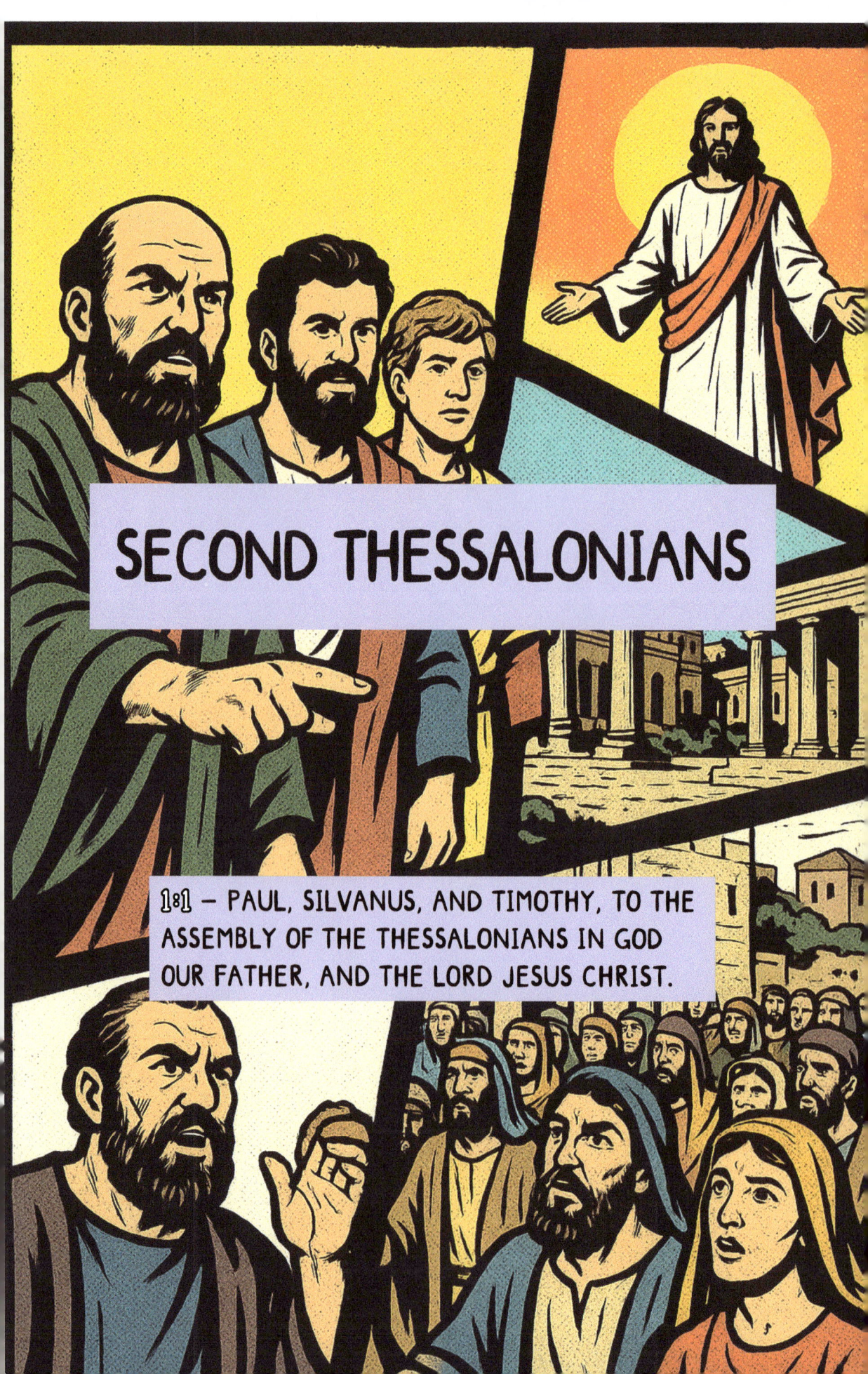

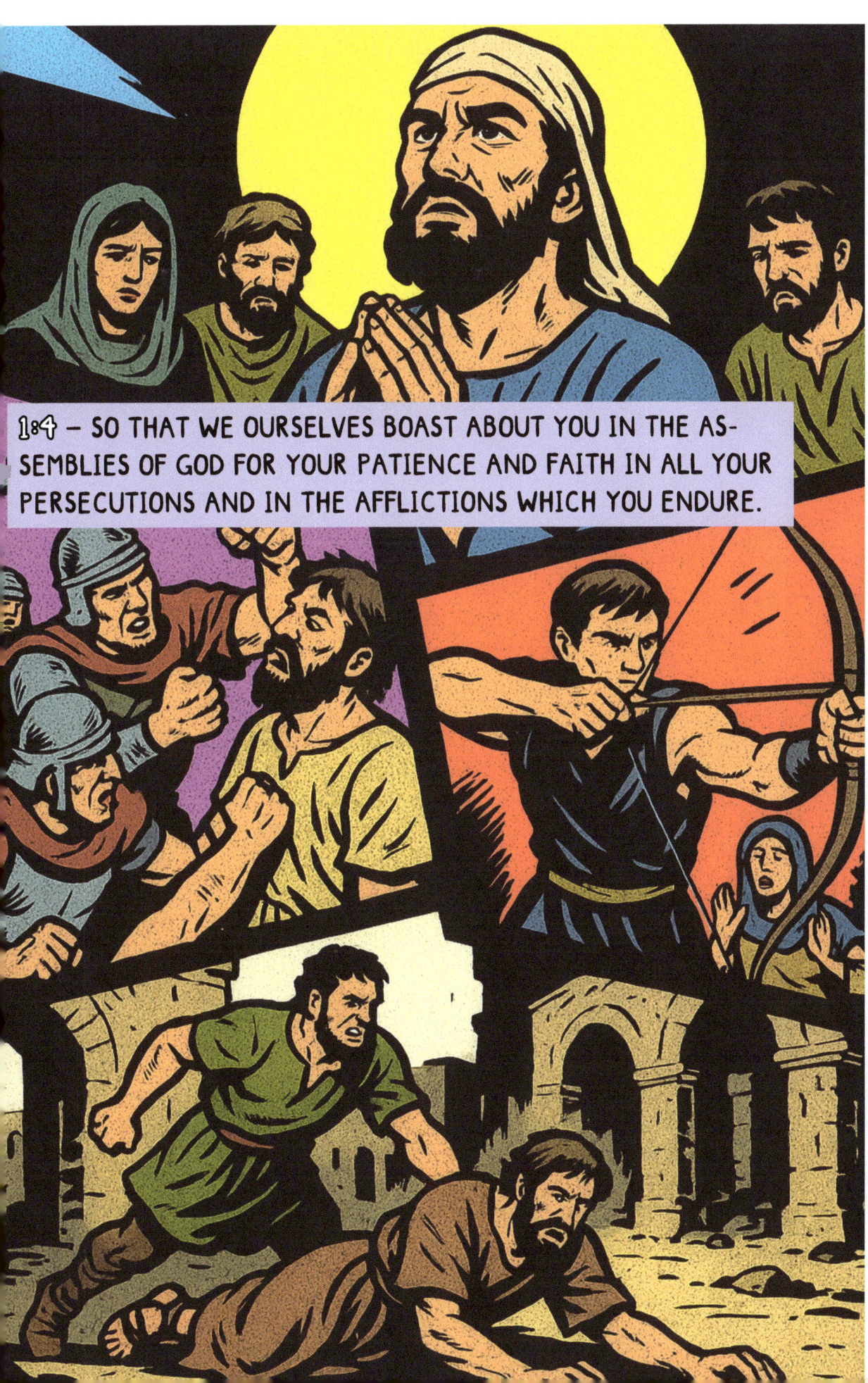

2:14 – TO WHICH HE CALLED YOU THROUGH OUR GOOD NEWS, FOR THE OBTAINING OF THE GLORY OF OUR LORD JESUS CHRIST.

3:11 – FOR WE HEAR OF SOME WHO WALK AMONG YOU IN REBELLION, WHO DON'T WORK AT ALL, BUT ARE BUSYBODIES.

www.ingramcontent.com/pod-product-compliance
Lightning Source LLC
Chambersburg PA
CBHW061117170426
43198CB00027B/3001